I0790792

ISLAMIC STRATEGIES TO LIVE A HAPPY AND PEACEFUL LIFE

Dr. Muddassir Khan

Introduction

Mental health problems affect all of us. The poor and the rich suffer. Young and old get depressed. Males and females are stressed. Muslims and non-Muslims have anxiety. No one is immune.

Allah says in the Quran, 'All living beings will taste death, and We will test you with evil and good situations, and to Us, you all will return.'

Allah blessed us with life and how we live it becomes us. On the Day of Judgment what happens to us depends on how we lived here.

Allah tests us with difficulties and ease. Good and bad happen. A person gets ill. Another is tested with her marriage. We suffer when our loved one suffers. All types of difficulties—financial, physical, and social—have an effect on our lives.

Even wealth, children, power, and social status are tests. An empty bank account causes us to worry but we also worry if it is in excess.

We can never be free of worries in this world. We are going to face problems; hence our focus should be on how to deal with them effectively. We should *solve* our problems but not get *dissolved* in them. Learning the strategies in this book helps us avoid complicating anxiety.

Live today as if it is Your Last Day

Live today as if it is your last day on Earth. It could be! We are not going to live here forever and we don't know when Allah has destined our death.

You will not postpone the things that you should be doing today for tomorrow—if today was your last. You will not think of calling your parents tomorrow. You will not wait another day to reconcile with your relatives. You will not be rude to your wife and child. You will not skip your prayers.

This attitude of living like it is your last day does not mean that you will not do things that take time to show a result. You will still do things that will have an impact tomorrow even if you were to die today.

The Prophet said that if a person is planting a seed and suddenly the Day of Judgment unfolds, he should continue planting the seed. This saying of the Prophet has a lot of wisdom. Even when the situation is chaotic and you know that the World is ending, it is recommended for a Muslim to still plant the seed knowing fully well that it will not grow. A Muslim is always optimistic and will be rewarded for his actions even if they do not cause the intended result.

So, even if today is your last day you will continue to work towards things that will only produce result after many days. You will continue to go to work and be a productive Muslim.

Even if today is your last day you will make preparation to go to Hajj next year. You will make plans for the holidays. You will make a detailed 'to do' list for the next few days or months. You will start learning Arabic even if today is your last day.

Living your life as if it was your last day will make you do things with *Ihsan* (excellence) and in the best possible way. The things that you do on your last day should be almost perfect.

The Prophet said, 'Pray like a man (who is) bidding farewell (like it is your last prayer), don't say things (today) that you'll have to apologize tomorrow, and give up the desire to acquire what people have.'

Prayer will be the first thing you will be questioned on the Day of Judgment. Imagine yourself praying the next compulsory prayer as if it was your last prayer. You will pray it with full concentration and attention. You will not worry about your work and family when praying. Praying like it is your last prayer will reduce your distractions. You cannot guarantee that you will be alive to pray the next prayer, so you should pray every prayer like it is your last.

If today is your last day you will avoid saying things to others that are painful. By avoiding hurtful talk now you will not have to apologize later. When having an argument we say the most hurtful things thinking that we will apologize later and reconcile. But there may not be a 'later' and you may die the very next moment. You don't want your last words to your parents, children, or spouse to be hurtful. When you are having a conversation, ask yourself, 'Will I be comfortable and happy if this was my last conversation with this person? Will Allah be pleased with this conversation?'

Don't go to bed with hatred towards someone. Don't go to bed after having an argument with someone. You may not wake up tomorrow. In Islam sleep is like death. Allah takes away our souls when we sleep and when we wake up they are returned back. So, we may die when we sleep if our souls are not returned. Before going to sleep apologize and reconcile. Even better than this is to avoid saying anything that will require an apology later.

Death is imminent. Make a bucket list. Do things that will benefit you even after your death. Ask forgiveness from Allah for all your sins. You may not have a tomorrow to repent.

Ibn Umar used to say, 'If you reach the evening then do not wait till the morning. If you reach the morning then do not wait till the evening. Take advantage of your health before you become sick, and of your life before your death.'

We should plan for tomorrow but not worry about tomorrow. You should worry about things that are under your control. This is similar to a farmer who digs the field and places the seeds. He has done his work and whether it will rain or not is beyond his power and control. So, he should not worry about rain. However, he can pray for beneficial rain and expect the best from Allah. You should do your work in the best possible way and leave it to Allah. There is no need to worry about the results. Worrying about the result will not change the result.

The Prophet said, 'If you rely on Allah as He should be relied on, (Allah) will provide you as the birds are provided. They (the birds) go out in morning hungry and return in the evening full (well fed).'

We must do our bit and struggle every day to get our provisions. Allah will give us if we have complete trust in Him.

Do not get angry

Two men were slandering each other in front of the Prophet. One of them got angry. This made him red in the face and the his veins became prominent. The Prophet said, 'I know a word which, if he says it—what he is feeling now will go away. If he said, "I seek refuge with Allah from the Shaitaan," what he is feeling (anger) will go away.'

Many emotions can give rise to anxiety and worry. Anger commonly causes anxiety. The severity of anger varies from rage at one extreme to being mildly irritated at the other.

Shaitaan employs various strategies to make you angry and commit sin. Some of these strategies are:

Labeling—Instead of looking at the person with both his good and bad qualities, Shaitaan makes you focus only on his bad qualities. You label him as a bad person and therefore justify being angry with him. This is a plot of Shaitaan.

Black or white thinking—This strategy is used by Shaitaan to make you see things and situations in extreme terms. You think that something very bad has happened. Actually, in life there are shades of gray and such Shaitaanic thoughts make us biased. We must try to understand whether there is any truth in their position before getting offended and angry at them.

Magnification—Shaitaan makes you magnify a small incident into something big and worthy of anger. Shaitaan increases your sense of being wronged.

To avoid Shaitaan making you angry, always say 'I seek refuge with Allah from Shaitaan.'

The Prophet said, 'If anyone gets angry and if he is standing, let him sit down, and his anger goes away. If it does not go away (even by sitting) then let him lie down.'

Whenever you get angry, you should relax by sitting down. Take a long, deep breath. Count slowly from one to ten before responding. This gives you a moment where you can think and choose your response.

Shaitaan wants you to react immediately and sin. But when you sit or lie down, you will calm down. You can think which strategy Shaitaan is using to make you angry.

We find many examples of a person striking and injuring someone or even killing him because of anger. Many divorce their wives in a moment of anger. By sitting down you prevent anger from getting out of control. A scholar commenting on this statement of the Prophet said, 'Standing is a position where a person can strike someone (become violent). By sitting a person is less likely to do this (indulge in violence and causing physical trauma).'

When a person asked the Prophet to advise him, The Prophet said, 'Do not become angry.' The man continued to ask the Prophet to advise him, and the Prophet continued to tell him, 'Do not become angry.' This man later contemplated on this advice of the Prophet and realized that anger combines all evils and should be avoided.

The Prophet once passed by a few people who were fighting. He was told they were wrestling and one of them can beat anybody in it. The Prophet said, 'Shall I not tell you (about the person) who is even stronger than him? He is a man who, when being mistreated by another, controls his anger. (By controlling his anger) He has defeated his own Shaitaan and also the Shaitaan of the one who had made him angry.'

Be Patient

We have been created by Allah and sent to this world in order to be tested. We are going to face happiness and sadness here and should be patient with these tests. Being patient will calm us. Allah rewards us for patience and by being patient we are successful in this life and in the hereafter. Allah helps us overcome the difficulty when we are patient.

Tests, problems, and obstacles are a part of our life. This should not make us miserable. We should accept that there will always be problems. With problems we grow.

Allah says, 'Surely, Allah is with those who are patient.'

You become more peaceful, and your worried thoughts and anxiety subside when you are patient. With patience we accept our problems and instead of worrying about them, we think of solutions to these problems. Patience makes us action-oriented.

Without patience we become irritable, and get annoyed easily. Simple things will begin to frustrate us if we are not patient.

When stuck in a traffic jam frustration will be of no benefit. Patience and remembering Allah will help. Take a deep breath at this time to help you relax. You may get late due to the traffic jam but by utilizing this time in remembrance of Allah—you earn good deeds.

According to Shaykh Uthaymeen, people respond in four ways to a major loss or calamity:

a) Anger: They get angry with Allah and become discontented with what Allah has destined and decreed for them. This leads to the unforgivable sin of disbelief.

Allah says, 'And among the people is he who worships Allah on an edge. If good touched him then is he is reassured by it. But if he is given a trial, then he turns on his face (to the other direction). He looses (both) this world and the Hereafter.'

Anger and discontent is expressed verbally and in physical actions such as becoming violent or by slapping one's own cheeks, shouting, and not listening to anyone else. So, when facing a calamity such as the death of a loved one we should avoid these actions.

b) Patience: This response though bitter and difficult, its outcome is sweeter than honey. Even if patience is burdensome and you dislike it, never become discontent. Keep on praising Allah.

c) Acceptance: This response if of a higher status than patience. For a person who accepts, both ease and hardship are the same. He accepts that everything happens by the will of Allah. We cannot control our emotional response to the calamity; and though we may feel sad when a calamity strikes, or happy in times of ease—we are completely pleased with our Lord. We accept that it is Allah who alternates the times of ease and hardship. Both are the same for us since we know that these are a result of the decree of Allah concerning us.

d) Gratitude: This is the best response to a calamity and is of the highest status. It shows that you are grateful to Allah for everything, including a calamity. You realize that greater calamities were possible. The calamity that affects your worldly interests is easier to bear than a calamity that affects your religion. Difficulties and hardships in this world are easier to bear than punishment in the hereafter. This hardship may be a way of reducing your sins and increasing your good deeds. You are therefore grateful to Allah for even the hardships and thank Allah for them.

The Prophet said, 'No worry, grief, or anything occurs to a believer but it becomes an expiation for him, (this applies to) even a thorn that pricks him.'

Happiness and sadness do not last forever. Though we want the pain to immediately disappear, it doesn't and will take time. You should, therefore, not struggle against what has been destined for you.

The Prophet said, 'The affair of the believer is amazing. He gets good in everything (in all situations) and this is only for the believer. If good happens to him, he expresses thankfulness (to Allah) and this (gratitude) is good for him. And if hardship comes his way, he endures it patiently and that (patience) is better for him.

We are our thoughts. If our thoughts are of gratitude to Allah—Allah will bless us. If we are patient and do not complain or blame Allah for our problems, then we are blessed. There is only goodness for the believers in all situations.

Allah says in the Quran, 'And be patient. Verily Allah is with those who are patient.'

Thoughts are just thoughts

We are not punished for bad thoughts.

The Prophet said, 'Allah decreed good and bad deeds. Whoever thinks of doing a good deed but does not do it, Allah will account for it one complete good deed. If he thinks and (also) does the good deed, Allah will write it down between ten and seven hundredfold or many more. If he thinks of doing a bad deed but does not do it, Allah will write it down as one complete good deed. And if he thinks and does the bad deed then Allah will write it down as one bad deed.'

The Prophet said, 'Allah, may He be exalted and glorified, will forgive my followers for what crosses their minds so long as they don't act upon them (such thoughts) or speak of it.'

The thoughts that worry you or trouble you are the evil whispers from Shaitaan. Ask Allah to protect you from such evil whispers.

You cannot stop having these thoughts but should allow the thoughts to pass through your mind without judging them or yourself. You are not a bad person if you get bad thoughts. Shaitaan is causing these thoughts to occur. He wants you to sin. If you fear Allah and don't do the sin, then Allah will write for you a good deed.

Ignoring these troublesome thoughts and not caring about them will help you stop worrying. We cannot control our thoughts but can only control whether we act on them. We will be answerable to Allah only for our actions.

If you get a thought such as, 'What will happen if I start sweating when giving a speech,' you should realize that this is just a thought and not a fact. And in case you do sweat then this is not the end of the world and everyone understands how stressful giving a talk is. You should, therefore, go ahead and give the speech or presentation even if you get these worrisome thoughts.

Such worrisome thoughts are from Shaitaan who wants to disable you so that you don't do any good deeds and become lazy and fearful. Being a Muslim your goal is to please Allah and you should do all the good deeds to achieve this goal. Don't let the thoughts from Shaitaan disable you.

When we are unhappy we get depressing thoughts. Such thoughts increase our unhappiness. When we realize that these thoughts are not true and ignore them—we become happier.

Bad thoughts are just thoughts—don't take them seriously.

Contemplate

Allah has commanded us to be attentive in our prayers and to read the Quran mindfully. Presence of mind and concentrating on the verses of the Quran brings a peaceful calm. We enjoy our worship when we contemplate the meaning of the verses of the Quran.

Mindfulness has become popular nowadays. There are various audio recordings available online that help us practice it. Breathing exercises are very popular. However, if we pray five times mindfully and read the Quran with contemplation, we don't need to do anything additional to achieve a state of mindfulness.

Contemplating helps us become better Muslims. We can contemplate on many things. We should contemplate on Allah's blessings and His Names and Attributes. All of Allah's creation, including our own body is worth contemplating. By contemplating on these topics we become amazed with the creation of Allah and praise Him. This helps us relax. We realize that Allah is our Lord and He is sustaining and providing for all of His creation. We should therefore not worry since He will also provide for us.

We should make time to contemplate our actions and worship. Are we doing the obligatory actions? What made us commit sin and how can we avoid it in future?

Contemplating will help us grow mentally. We analyse our actions and implement strategies that help us nurture our soul and body.

Ibn Al Qayyim said, 'The more a person contemplates over the shortness of this life and its temporary nature, the harder he will work and the more effort he will exert. Contemplation will make him utilize his time to the optimum.'

Ibn Abbas said, 'Contemplating over the good deeds makes a person to (want to) perform them (even more), and contemplating over evil drives a person to avoid it.'

Al-Fudhayl, said, 'Contemplation acts like a mirror and shows one his faults and good qualities.'

Contemplating the status of Muslims today will make you teary. Your problems will appear to be small when you compare them to what Muslims are facing today.

A few minutes every day—preferably in the morning— we should think about deeds that benefit us in the Hereafter. We should contemplate about the things that cause us harm in the hereafter and how to avoid them. Contemplating over the hereafter will increase your wisdom and revive your heart. You will realize that the problems of this world cannot be compared to what can possibly happen in the hereafter when a person does not obey Allah and His messenger.

Contemplating the favors of Allah upon you will make you peaceful. When you compare the numerous blessings of Allah to the unpleasant things that have occurred to you then you will see how they are extremely small in comparison to the blessings of Allah.

Contemplating on the suffering of others will make you realize how you have been favoured over others.

The Prophet said, 'Look at those who are below you (in worldly positions), and do not look at those that are above you (in worldly positions).'

Put your trust in Allah

Only Allah knows what will happen in the future. We don't know and only hope for the best. Worrying about our problems is no guarantee that the future will become better. In fact, what we worry about the future rarely happens.

Even the Prophets don't know the future and this is illustrated in the story of Musa. Once Musa and Khidr wanted to go to the other side of the river and asked the owners of a ship—who were fishermen—to help them. The fishermen agreed to help them even without payment. While crossing the river, Khidr made a small hole in the hull of the ship and damaged it. Musa could not understand why Khidr did this. We come to know the wisdom of Khidr's strange actions only later.

The ship belonged to a group of poor fishermen and their King was tyrannical. He was confiscating every single usable ship. He was oppressing his people and taking their ships by force. By putting a small hole in the ship Khidr made sure that the ship was not in service but could be repaired later. This ship was, therefore, not confiscated. By damaging the ship, Khidr was, in fact, saving the ship. The poor fishermen were generous and had allowed them to ride for free. They were kind-hearted and did a lot of good actions. They showed their generosity through the ship and Allah, therefore, preserved the vehicle of their generosity.

Imagine the immediate frustration of the fisherman when they realized that their ship had been damaged. Imagine their anger when they realized that this damage was caused by the people who they had given a free ride. But later in the future also imagine them seeing the King confiscate the ship of every single fisherman in the entire city except their ship. Their frustration would instantaneously change into happiness and they would praise Allah that He sent someone to destroy their ship. This is because just like all human beings, the fishermen were being short sighted and only looking at the next five minutes. They did not realize the wisdom in their loss. They didn't realize that this calamity was protecting them from a much bigger calamity.

Allah is taking care of us even when we are having problems. So the next time you suffer financial loss, the next time you're in a car accident, the next time damage happens, do remember the story of the fishermen and then put your trust in Allah. Thank Allah that whatever happened wasn't worse and acknowledge that Allah has the right to do as He pleases. Also pray to Allah to make the situation better. This is the attitude of the believer.

Allah says in the Quran, 'If you are suffering hardships, (realize that) they too are suffering similar hardships. But you hope from Allah that for which they hope not.'

<u>Forgive</u>

One of the most beautiful aspect of Islam is to forgive others and having a clean heart towards our fellow believers. We should not only forgive but also forget. We should forgive the grudges that we have with others. Our heart should be free from jealousy, retribution, enmity, hatred, revenge, and anger. Remove all these evil things from your heart to have a peaceful and calm life filled with happiness and love. Give the person another chance. Turn over a new leaf.

When we study the life of the Prophet (peace and blessings of Allah be upon him) we get to know that he had many opportunities to exact revenge on those who did him wrong, but he forgave.

The Quran reminds us that it is the characteristic of a Muslim to forgive. A Muslim is forgiving towards his fellow Muslims. He overlooks their faults.

This forgiveness is of a higher priority when it comes to our family. We come to know this when we study the life of Prophet Yusuf. His brothers tried to kill him when he was a child. Allah saved him. Later when he became a powerful minister he could have easily punished them, but he forgave them. He forgave them to such an extent that he did not even blame them but blamed Shaitaan for making them commit this sin.

When you hold grudges, animosity, anger, hatred, and resentment against someone—you are acknowledging that this person has power over you. You are still suffering from what happened long back. You are holding on to these negative emotions which are eating your heart and disturbing your sleep and health. For your heart to heal and for you to be at peace with yourself—you should forgive and forget. Move on with your life. Let go of the resentment. Enjoy your life.

When you forgive others, Allah will forgive you!

Allah says, 'Forgive and pardon. Don't you love that Allah should forgive you? And Allah is often Forgiving, Most Merciful.'

Believe in Destiny

What if this happens?
What if that happens?

A person continues to worry about the future.

We also worry about things that happened in the past. We continue to wonder whether if we had done something else we could have avoided this problem.

Our mind continues to ask us what we will do in case this or that happens. Our mind wants reassurance that everything will be alright. This reassurance can only be provided if we have faith in destiny.

What happened and what will happen are known to Allah and have already been written and destined for us.

Allah says in the Quran—Say; 'No evil will fall on us except that which Allah has meant for us (to happen). He is our Lord.'

The problems we face are destined to happen. Problems that are not destined will never occur. We should live in the present without having any excess worry about the past or the future. We should believe in destiny and expect the best from Allah.

Allah says, 'No difficulty occurs on the earth or in yourselves but is inscribed in the Book (of destiny), before We bring it into existence. Verily, this is easy for Allah. (This is) In order that you should not be sad over the matters that you fail to get, nor exult over those that have been given to you. And Allah does not love the arrogant boaster.'

Faith in destiny makes us realize that what we did or did not get has already been written. We should, therefore, not be sad. Also, what we gained or were blessed with was also written. Therefore, the good thing that happened to us was from Allah and therefore we should not boast that our hard work or intelligence caused it to happen.

Prophet (peace and blessings of Allah be upon him) said, 'Everything has a reality about it. The slave does not reach the real faith until he knows what has reached him (happiness or sorrow) was not going to miss him and what has missed him was not going to reach him.'

Prophet said, 'Allah is more compassionate towards his slave than a mother is towards her child.'

Everything that Allah decrees for us is in our best interest. Allah has destined what is best for us and we will come to know this only in the end and not now when we are facing problems.

Allah says in the Quran that Allah does not burden a soul more than it can bear. Allah has more confidence in us and only gives us problems that we can handle. However, we human beings are weak and when faced with a problem we put up our hands, start worrying, and say this is too much! It is not too much and you can handle all the problems that Allah gives you. Allah will not give you a problem that you cannot handle. All praise is to Allah!

<u>How to deal with others</u>

A Muslim is beneficial to others. He thinks of ways he can help and reduce their burden. We can do good to others with good deeds and by kind words.

Throughout the day beginning from when you wake up, ask yourself, 'How can I help someone today?' Your intention when helping others should be to please Allah and you should not expect anything in return from them. Even if no one notices your act of kindness you know with certainty that Allah will reward you.

Allah says in the Quran, 'Whoever does a *good deed*, male or female, and is a *believer*, We will *bless him with a good life*, and in the hereafter, they will be rewarded (compensated) for the good deeds they used to do.'

A believer who does good and righteous deeds is blessed by Allah with a good and pure life in this world.

Helping others gives us peace of mind. Our hearts get softer when we see others in difficulty and help them. It makes us appreciate the blessings of Allah.

The Prophet said, 'If you want to make your heart soft then feed the poor and wipe your hand over the head of the orphan.'

The Prophet said, 'The most beloved person to Allah is he who brings most benefit to people, and the most beloved action to Allah is that you bring happiness to a fellow Muslim, or relieve him of distress.'

Even if you can only make others smile it is considered to be charity and will be written as a good deed in your record. The one who makes others happy is also the one who is happy.

Become easygoing. Keep smiling even in the face of difficulties. Don't be uptight and make difficult rules for yourself and others. Allow things to go in a way that is not according to your plan. Let go of your expectations. Allow yourself and others to make mistakes.

If someone is late to a meeting try to understand the reason. Don't assume the worst and give him the serious look. Don't be frustrated with him but smile at him. He is a human and no human is perfect.

Be humorous but always tell the truth. Don't tell a lie to make others laugh.

The Prophet said, 'Woe to the one who lies to make people laugh. Woe to him.'

Ibn Umar was asked, 'Did the companions of the Prophet laugh?' He replied, 'Yes, and they had faith in their hearts like mountains.'

Once an old lady came to the Prophet and requested him, 'Please pray for me that I go to heaven.'
The Prophet replied, 'Have you not heard? Old women cannot go to heaven.'
The old lady was upset on hearing this. The Prophet smiled and explained to the old lady in a pleasant manner that she will become young before being sent to paradise. She will go to heaven but as a young person. She was very happy to hear this and cheered up.

We depend on each other in this world for our needs. We should always try to help others with what we have. Be beneficial to others and Allah will bless you.

Prophet said, 'The best of mankind is the one that brings the most benefit to the rest of mankind.'

Help others even before they ask. But don't expect them to help you. Don't desire thanks and gratitude from any human being. Only expect from Allah. This is because if others don't help you according to your expectations you start complaining and this creates discord. Your relationship will be affected and your mental peace will be disturbed. If you have no expectations from others but still if someone helps you, then your love for this person will increase.

Allah says in the Quran, '(They say): We feed you for only the sake of Allah. No reward do we desire from you, not even thanks.'

Always think about what rights we are not fulfilling. Don't think about what rights others are not fulfilling. You won't be asked about them on the Day of Judgment but will only be asked about your actions.

Have a strong relationship with Allah. Expect everything from Allah. Allah will give you and fulfil all your needs.

Many misunderstandings can be resolved by honest communication instead of being silent and allowing Shaitaan to put bad thoughts in your mind.

It is not possible to be at peace with yourself if you blame others. Blaming others will restrict the development of your personality. You will never analyse whether what you did was suboptimal or wrong. You will always think that it was someone else's fault and this will impede your mental and physical growth.

Even if the other person was obviously wrong, you should not hold them accountable for your happiness. You are responsible for your happiness. By blaming him you drain your mental energy and create stress for yourself.

We cannot know someone's intention. We can judge only their actions. Probably they did something with a good intention even if it hurt you. Always clarify from someone why they did something instead of assuming that they had the worst intentions.

Enmity will destroy your peace of mind. Your enemy will occupy your mind and disturb you. Is the enmity worth it? Can you let go? Holding grudges blocks happiness.

Allah says, 'And if you are patient and become Al-Muttaqun (the pious), there cunningness will not cause you even the least harm. Surely, Allah encompasses their actions.'

Allah says, 'And the evil plot only affects the person who makes it.'

Pray for your enemy since Allah can guide anyone. Let go of the hatred and relax.

The Prophet said, 'The diseases of the previous nations have affected you—envy and hatred. These are the destroyers and destroy the Deen (religion). By the one in whose hand my soul is, you will never enter Paradise until you have faith and you will never believe until you love each other. Should I not direct you to that which—when you do it—(you) will establish this (love for each other) within you? Spread Salam (greetings of Peace) amongst yourselves.'

The Prophet said, 'Be soft in enmity with your enemy since maybe someday he will become your close friend.'

Don't be excessively harsh with your enemy. Have patience. Give time and avoid acting in haste.

Be happy with yourself and the things that you have. Stop comparing yourself with others. For example, a person has a mobile which he is very happy to own. He looks after it and keeps it clean. But when he sees his friend having the latest iPhone, he becomes jealous. Due to jealousy he stops appreciating the phone which he was happy to have and his happiness is reduced.

Another example is when you give your son a chocolate. He is very happy and satisfied. Later when you give your daughter two chocolates the happiness of your son is affected. He is no longer happy. He still has the chocolate that made him happy a few minutes back but the same chocolate no longer makes him happy now.

We should be content with what we have and we don't require what others have to enjoy our life.

The Prophet said, 'People will be on goodness until they don't envy one another.'

We should be happy with the blessings that Allah has given to us and others. Envy and feeling jealous are actually complaining to Allah and should be avoided. We should compete with others for the best in the hereafter and not for the things in this world. We should utilize our energy in the correct way and not waste it by feeling jealous.

Allah says, 'Allah increases the provision for whom He wills, and reduces it (for whom He wills), and they rejoice in the life of this world, whereas the life of this world when compared to the hereafter is only a brief passing enjoyment.'

You should mind your own business and should only correct others when they are doing a thing which is against the principles of Islam.

Prophet Muhammad said, '(A) Part of the Perfection of One's Islam is him leaving that (thing) which does not concern him.'

By doing this you will free up a lot of your energy and time. If two relatives are fighting, don't interfere and worsen the fight. You should interfere only if you are able to make reconciliation between them. If someone is backbiting and you are not able to stop him then leave the gathering after saying 'Peace'.

You should ignore things which don't concern you or impact your life. This also applies to Facebook, WhatsApp, Instagram, and other social apps. Don't get involved in unnecessary arguments and waste your time and energy.

Why did he say this? What made her take this action? Don't allow thoughts of anger and enmity towards someone overwhelm you. Try to understand why your friend or relative said or did something that you didn't like. Develop compassion towards them even if what they did was obviously wrong. Don't judge their actions. It is possible that you would have done the same in their situation. Develop loving-kindness towards them.

Being genuinely eager to know why they said or acted in this way will make you calm and less annoyed. It will break the cycle of negative thoughts that Shaitaan is cycling in your brain. This will put a brake on the unhealthy thoughts.

Maintaining relationships is not optional but compulsory in Islam.

Instead of saying or thinking, 'How disgusting of him to react in this way considering all the favors that I have done to him,' think or say to yourself, 'Maybe he was under intense pressure to do this thing because of the problems that he is facing. May Allah guide all of us.'

Even in the case of strangers understanding why they are being harsh and rude will help you calm down. You may be stuck in a traffic jam and the vehicle behind you is honking continuously asking you to move ahead. Instead of getting irritated and thinking, 'Can't he see that the vehicle in front of me is not moving,' think, 'this guy may have an important meeting to attend,' or, 'he may have someone in the car who needs urgent medical treatment.' Thinking in this way will reduce your tension and help you relax. Always take a deep breath and say 'I seek refuge in Allah from Shaitaan.'

In a conversation, if someone says a thing that you don't agree with—don't interrupt him. Let him explain it completely. And even after completely listening to him if you still don't agree with him then you can say that you don't agree with his point of view. And since you were kind and listened to him completely, he will now give you time to explain your position.

The Prophet said, 'A believing man (husband) should not hate a believing woman (his wife). If he dislikes one of her characteristic, he will like another.' This saying of the Prophet has many lessons for us on how to deal with others. We should accept the fact that all persons have imperfections. We should concentrate on their good qualities and overlook their bad qualities.

Repent and Seek Help from Allah

Allah says in the Quran, 'O you who believe! Ask for help through patience and prayer. Verily, Allah is with those who are patient.'

If there is a problem, we should accept it patiently without complaining or becoming angry. After this we should seek solutions to the problem. We should also ask Allah to help us solve the problem and to have mercy on us. Doing this with folded hands and crying when asking Allah will reduce your pain and will make you feel light and calm. Since you have asked the Creator of the heavens and earth to help you there is no need to worry.

Along with asking from Allah we have to work hard and earnestly to get what we asked. Praying should go along with action.

The Prophet said, 'Strive (work hard and be eager) for what will benefit you, and seek the help of Allah, and do not be lazy. And if something afflicts you, do not say, 'If I had done such and such, then such and such would have happened.' But say, 'This is the decree of Allah, He does what He wills.' This is because (saying) 'if' opens the door to Shaitaan.'

Whenever the Prophet was afflicted with a trial causing stress or sorrow, he would say, 'O Living and Eternal Maintainer! I seek help by Your Mercy!'

Allah is ever living and always dependable. We should ask Him for help instead of human beings who may or may not help. Allah always responds to the *Dua* (prayer) of the believer. He is merciful and is always eager to listen to your prayers.

Sins cause mental stress and disturbance. Breaking the laws of Allah is a source of unrest and tension in our soul. It is possible that the difficulties we are facing are a punishment for our sins. Sins invite punishment from Allah and this can occur in this world itself.

Your reaction and feelings to something are an excellent way to know that the thing that you are planning to do is pleasing to Allah or not. Everyone has an internal moral compass. Our conscience has an important role to play in our life. It can recognize what is good and what is evil.

The Prophet said, 'Righteousness is (having a) good character and sins are those that cause disturbance in your heart and you hate for people to find out about it.'

The Prophet said, 'If you are happy with your good deeds and if your evil deeds make you sad, then you are a believer.'

Sins make us feel bad and we are troubled by it. We should give up all the things that make us feel bad spiritually since they disturb our heart.

The Prophet (peace and blessings of Allah be upon him) said, 'Leave (those things) that makes you doubt for that which does not make you have any doubt. Verily, truth brings peace of mind and falsehood sows doubt.'

The Prophet said, 'Verily, a black spot appears in the heart of a believer when he commits a sin. If he repents and does not do the sin again, and seeks forgiveness, then his heart is polished (the black spot is removed). But if he does the sin again then the blackness increases.'

Having sins is like walking with a heavy weight and this causes enormous stress. Repenting relieves the stress, wipes out the sins, and makes you feel light and relaxed.

The Prophet said, 'The one whose preoccupation is the hereafter, Allah places freedom from want in his heart, corrects his affairs, and the worldly things come to him humiliated. And whoever makes the World his preoccupation then Allah places poverty in front of his eyes, makes his affairs difficult, and nothing of the world will come to him except that which was already written for him.'

Allah says, 'The good and the evil action cannot be equal. Repel (the evil) with something better. Then (you will see) he who was your enemy (has now become) is now as though your close friend. But no one is given (the above qualities) except the ones who are patient, and no one is granted it (these qualities) except those who have a mighty good fortune.'

Always remember Allah in all situations. Remembrance of Allah brings tranquillity to the heart and removes worry.

Allah says in the Quran, 'In the remembrance of Allah do hearts find satisfaction.'

May Allah bless you with a happy and peaceful life. Jazak Allahu Khair for reading this book.